Should anyone try to join the four points of the European continent extended furthest to the East, to the West, to the North and to the South with straight lines, the lines would intersect near the heart of Poland. Owing to landscape diversity, convoluted paths of history and its location in the heart of Europe, Poland is an attractive country, worthy of in-depth exploration. In this work we aim to present Poland, as it is – **a country on the crossroads**.

Brudzieński Landscape Park is located near Płock and along the Vistula.

POLAND

POLAND

A country on the crossroads

Christian Parma

photography

Maciej Krupa

text

✳ Wydawnictwo PARMA® PRESS

Any country – including your own native-land – can be viewed from various perspectives. An assessment performed by a geographer or a statistics specialist would seem most common and objective. Such an interpretation typically depicts Poland as a country covering an area of 312 thousand sq. km, one of the biggest European states. A home to over 38 million citizens, of whom 24 million are city-dwellers and just over 14 million chose to settle in rural areas. A country, where for each 100 males there lives 106 females; where 10% of the citizens have graduated from universities and around 33% completed their secondary education. One might also add that Poland enjoys unrestricted access to the sea, that it borders with 7 countries, its territory is divided into 16 provinces and over 2500 communes. That the Seym, being supervised by the Senate, governs the state, and that the President acts as head of state – consequently the Republic of Poland exemplifies a parliamentary democracy. A myriad of figures and data may be quoted at this point, we could sketch maps and enclose charts. Still, it doesn't have to be that way...

For Poland is also a sunrise admired from the seashore; the aroma of forest after rainfall when the sun hanging low over the horizon struggles to pierce down through the branches; it is the Wawel castle gloriously towering over the curve of Vistula river; and the magnificent snow-capped Tatra Mountains observed from the peaks of Turbacz or Babia Góra. Poland is languid windings and overflows of the Biebrza river, Cracow's Franciscan basilica's dim interior lit up by stained-glass windows designed by Wyspiański, mighty oaks and European bison of Białowieża, narrow alleys of Kazimierz-upon-Vistula and the white waters of Dunajec fighting its way across the Pieniny Mountains. Cracow's Main Market Square and the Old Town of Warsaw; minuscule wooden Orthodox churches in Beskid Niski and the synagogues of the past surviving in the Cracow's district of Kazimierz; poetry of Zbigniew Herbert and Father Baka, music by Henryk Mikołaj Górecki and Bartuś Obrochta, grand canvasses by Jan Matejko and dream-like paintings by Witkacy; Veit Stoss's altar and Our Lady of Krużlowa, little church in Dębno and the basilica in Licheń. Multitude in diversity.

For centuries Polish literature stood on the fringes of the grand literatures: the French, the German, the English and the Russian. In the Polish literary tradition it is poetry that enjoys greatest significance; prose has never achieved such level of universality, nor has any Polish novel ever joined the club of European classics. Four Poles so far have been awarded a Nobel Prize for literature – Henryk Sienkiewicz (1905), Władysław Reymont (1924), Czesław Miłosz (1980) and Wisława Szymborska (1996). Stanisław Ignacy Witkiewicz "Witkacy", the author of novels and plays staged world-wide, was a visionary ahead of his time. Similarly, Witold Gombrowicz was a truly original and universally appreciated writer. But it is poetry that the Polish contemporary literature rests upon, with Miłosz, Szymborska, Zbigniew Herbert and Tadeusz Różewicz being its brightest stars in the firmament.

Veit Stoss's altar in St. Mary's Church in Cracow remains the most outstanding achievement of Polish Gothic tradition. Nonetheless, the Polish Gothic and Renaissance manifest themselves predominantly via masterpieces of architecture. Historical architecture, sacral for the most part, proves to be inspired chiefly by Baroque influences. Canaletto's paintings praise the glory of the 18th century Warsaw, Marcello Baciarelli and Piotr Norblin with their inclination for historical and social themes in graphic arts laid foundations for the Polish national art. The 19th century witnessed a flourish of Polish painting, marked by the works of Piotr Michałowski, Wojciech Gerson, the Gierymscy brothers and, to greatest extent, Jan Matejko. At the turn of the 20th century the period of Młoda Polska (Young Poland) prevailed on the Polish artistic arena featuring Stanisław Wyspiański, Józef Mehoffer, Leon Wyczółkowski and Jacek Malczewski. That is when the "zakopiański" style in architecture and design came into being, introduced by its creator – Stanisław Witkiewicz. Among the artists actively operating in the inter-war period the names of Tadeusz Makowski and Zbigniew Pronaszko deserve particular attention, as well as a Paris-seated team of painters representing the Capists school, and a marvel on his own rights – S. I. Witkiewicz "Witkacy", son of Stanisław, the originator of "zakopiański" style. In the second half of the 20th century Tadeusz Brzozowski and Władysław Hasior seemed of foremost significance for Polish art. Currently it is Magdalena Abakanowicz who enjoys greatest esteem among art connoisseurs worldwide.

Frederic Chopin continues to be the sole representative of Polish romantic composition with a household name in all corners of the world. The works of Karol Szymanowski, however, seem to be gaining in popularity as well. The circle of contemporary composers, whose music enjoys international appreciation, embraces Henryk Mikołaj Górecki, the author of the popular Third Symphony. The compositions by Witold Lutosławski and Krzysztof Penderecki have also reached international concert halls. Music connoisseurs all over the world are well acquainted with artistic achievements of Wojciech Kilar and Zbigniew Preisner – mainly due to their involvement in composing sound-track music. For many years the pianist Krystian Zimmerman, has enjoyed warm reception by international audience in the finest concert halls of the world. Tomasz Stańko is perceived to be one of the greatest jazz trumpeters of all time and the works of the late pianist and composer Krzysztof Komeda are invariably recognised and cherished.

Greatest international repute among Polish film makers is ascribed to Roman Polański, for many years working abroad, the director of "Nóż w wodzie" ("A Knife in the Water"), "Chinatown", "Tess", and the laureate of Palm d'Ore of the Cannes Film Festival for "The Pianist". The only Polish director ever to have been awarded an honorary Oscar for lifetime achievements is Andrzej Wajda, the prominent representative of a so-called "Polish School" in filmmaking. Movies by Krzysztof Kieślowski are also appreciated world-wide, similarly documentaries by Marcel Łoziński and Andrzej Fidyk.

The two names of Polish theatrical personalities popular abroad are Tadeusz Kantor, the founder of Cricot 2 Theatre in Cracow, and Jerzy Grotowski – originator and animator of the Wrocław Laboratorium Theatre. Konrad Swinarski of Teatr Stary (the Old Theatre) in Cracow and his unforgettable staging of "Dziady" by Adam Mickiewicz definitely deserve mentioning at this point. Currently, the name of Poland is extolled abroad due to the activity of alternative theatres, among them Gardzienice established by Włodzimierz Staniewski and Teatr Ósmego Dnia (The Theatre of the Eighth Day) from Poznań.

Should anyone try to join the four points of the European continent extended furthest to the East, to the West, to the North and to the South with straight lines, the lines would intersect at the heart of Poland. For Poland has been located on the crossroads of Europe centuries long. To the Russians our country used to be, and still remains to be perceived as the vestibule of the West, for France and Germany it is a presage of the distressing East. For centuries it was a bulwark of Western Christianity and concurrently the asylum of religious tolerance. Polish territory has survived innumerable armed conflicts, including the two World Wars. In the 16th century the Polish kingdom was a European power, two centuries later as a result of tragic entanglements it was erased from the map of Europe for the lengthy 123 years. A short period of stability in the inter-war period was followed by the catastrophes of Nazi occupation and the Soviet domination. Freedom and democracy resumed in 1989. Poland regained access to political and economical structures of the united Europe.

For centuries, Roman and Byzantine influences overlapped in Poland. It is here that basilicas and Orthodox churches were erected, Jewish culture flourished and bore fruit of everlasting value. Cities were seated in compliance with German law, and Queen Bona, of Italian descent, laid foundations to Polish Renaissance. This is where Copernicus, Marie Skłodowska-Curie and the Nobel Peace Prize laureate Lech Wałęsa were born and active. Here we find the birthplace of Pope John Paul II, who did so very much to change the face of our world.

Poles are relatively immobile; they do not travel extensively and if so – they tend to be better acquainted with the monuments of Rome and the seashores of Greece than the enchanting nooks of their native land. Let's take the liberty to pronounce the most banal statement – Poland is an exciting, wonderful and picturesque country. We may not have as many monuments and churches as the Italians, as many castles as the French, mountains as the Swiss or beaches as the Greeks do, but owing to landscape diversity, convoluted paths of history and its location in the heart of Europe, Poland is an attractive country, worthy of in-depth exploration. In this work we aim to present Poland as it is – a country on the crossroads.

← The Malbork Castle. Piece of sculptured ornaments of the Golden Gate portal (High Castle) depicting the Imprudent Maidens.

Wooded overflow-arms of the Vistula River in the vicinity of Secymin (Mazovia). → →

Słowiński National Park has been included by UNESCO into the World Biosphere Reserve.
Movable sand-dunes astound visitors.

← A storm at Słowiński National Park uncovers forest that grew here 3000 years ago.

The River Biebrza meanders through fens and overgrown marshes. →→

The Suwałki region intrigues with varied moraine landscape carved by the retreating glacier.

The Czarne (Black) Lake in Olsztyńskie Lake District. →

Białowieża Forest, part of the Białowieża National Park →→
designated by UNESCO as a Biosphere Reserve.

Poland's grandest river – the Vistula – winding along its broad riverbed near Płock.

The picturesque Bug Floodplain can be admired less than 20 km → out from the northern edges of Warsaw.

Szydłów region. Remarkable forms of weathering sandstone rocks – Skałki Piekło (Hell Rocks), natural reserve. →→

Poppies – this ubiquitous weed of Mazovian fields adds to the charm of local homesteads.

← The vicinity of Rozalin. Birch woods prevail in the boggy areas of Mazovia.

Pałuki, the land at the north-eastern frontiers of Wielkopolska, is the region of fertile fields stretching far beyond the horizon.

The Góreckie Lake in Wielkopolski National Park. →

Jabłeczna village in Podlasie region, only several kilometres away from the Belarusian border. Willows at the side of the village road.

← Jeziorzany in Lublin region. Riverside pastures on the bank of Wieprz, one of the right-hand side tributaries of the Vistula River.

In the Jelenia Góra area of Lower Silesia, the view from the foot of Chojnik Castle. → →

Potok Złoty (Golden Stream). This natural limestone bridge, known as Brama Twardowskiego
(Twardowski Gateway), is hidden deep in the seclusion of thick forests.

Ogrodzieniec. Limestone rocks prevailing in the landscape of Jura Krakowsko-Częstochowska. →

Beskid Wyspowy. Towards the peak of Paprotnia hill weathering processes of sandstone rocks
led to the formation of stone blocks labelled The Brodziński Stones.

The Western Bieszczady Mountains. The renowned and much-visited →
massif of Połonina Wetlińska, which peaks at 1255 m Roh.

Spis in Małopolska region. Undulating hills and narrow strips of plough-land combine to form remarkably picturesque vista.

The panorama of Dunajec in Pieniński National Park as observed from Sokolica. →

The Tatra Mountains towering over the villages of Podhale, viewed from the settlement of Sierockie in Pogórze Gubałowskie. →→

Turbary reserve area of Bór na Czerwonem near Nowy Targ.

The smoke from a bonfire float on the air among haystacks of Bukowina Tatrzańska. →

The Tatras. In the spring crocus or saffron is ubiquitous on the Tatra glades.

← The High Tatras. Czarnostawiańska Siklawa – the waterfall cascading into the tarn of Morskie Oko.

The High Tatras. Niżnie Rysy surrounded by clouds and Turnia Zwornikowa viewed from Dolina za Mnichem. → →

The High Tatras. The peaks of Kościelec and Świnica in their winter attire towering over Gąsienicowa Valley.

Subalpine forest in the High Tatras. →

Zakopane. Krupówki – Poland's most renowned pedestrian route.

Kazimierz Dolny, magnificent site on the banks of the Vistula River. Viewed from Krzyżowa Mountain. →

Zamość. Arcades of 17th century houses in the Great Market Square remind of Italian architectural patterns of the Renaissance period. → →

Wrocław. Gothic City Hall from the 14ᵗʰ-15ᵗʰ century with its richly ornamented facades and a tower of rising 66 metres high.

← Brzeg in Silesia. The panorama of the city as observed from the City Hall tower towards the castle and the Baroque Church of the Elevation of the Holy Cross.

Kłodzko. The Gothic-style stone bridge over the Młynówka is considered by some to resemble a mini-version of Prague's Charles →→
Bridge. It links Sand Island with the Old Town. The Baroque sculpturework was funded by local burghers in the 18th century.

Bydgoszcz. The 19th-century Lloyd Mansion and contemporary "New Granaries" (*Nowe Spichrze*) form the backdrop
for Jerzy Buczkowski's "Three Graces". Put in place in 1989, the goddesses Thalia (the cheerful), Aglaea (the splendid)
and Euphrosyne (the mirthful) imbue the banks of the Brda with a fine atmosphere.

Toruń. The Neo-Renaissance Artus House dating back to the end of the 19th century. →

Gdańsk, a seat to the ancient harbour and one of Poland's most exquisite group of historic →→
monuments – the Long Market with the panorama of the City Hall.

Chojnice, the city located at the outskirts of Bory Tucholskie (Tucholskie Primeval Forests).
Market Square with Neo-Gothic city hall.

Warsaw, Old Town Market Square. The bevelled corner of the Simonetti family house is adorned →
with decorative clock and a plate commemorating the Square's restoration.

Warsaw. The view of a new icon of the capital – the 192-metre apartment block
known as "The Sail", which was designed by Daniel Libeskind.

Warsaw. City centre as viewed from the Siekierkowski Bridge. →

Łódź. The city's main street – Piotrkowska. The artery is 4 km long, of which the majority is closed to vehicular traffic.

← Iłża. The panorama of the city perpetuating medieval architectural plans. Viewed from the bishop's castle.

Gniezno. The cathedral and Tumska Street admired from the Main Market Square.

Leszno. Burghers' houses raised in the 18th and the 19th century. →

Poznań. City Hall, the Renaissance Grand Vestibule with the polychromatic ceiling in low relief. The chamber is also known as the Renaissance Hall. →→

Niedzica. Fortified castle of mixed Gothic and Renaissance styles overlooks the artificial lake of Czorsztyn.

Cracow, the Wawel Castle – courtyard with arcade cloisters in Renaissance style. →

Przemyśl-Bakończyce. Prince Hieronim Lubomirski had his Eclectic palace put up here, →→
taking building material from the walls of the old 17th-century castle.

Ujazd – remnants of the Krzyżtopór castle following the Mannerist style.

Ogrodzieniec. Picturesque ruins of the Late-Gothic/Renaissance castle on Janowskiego Mountain. →

Moszna near Opole. Courtyard of an eclectic castle erected in the late 19ᵗʰ century.

← Książ. Elements of the Renaissance southern facade of the castle, above the Chestnut Terrace.

Pszczyna. Baroque manor house rebuilt in the late 19ᵗʰ century. The Mirror Hall is fitted with two →→
enormous mirrors; the surface of each of them amounts to 14 sq. meters.

PETROF

Zagórze Śląskie. A piece of scratch-work ornaments of the gateway building in the Grodno castle.

← Sucha. Originally Gothic, but frequently reconstructed, castle of Czoch – former seat of the Dukes of Świdnica.

Szczecin. The Castle of Pomeranian Dukes. Its walls are topped with Renaissance attic and the Clock Tower protruding from the wall face. →→

Lidzbark Warmiński, square Gothic castle with a courtyard and four corner towers.

Malbork. The castle was erected between the 13ᵗʰ and the 15ᵗʰ century. It is perceived to be →
one of the most exquisite examples of medieval stronghold architecture.

Białystok. Graceful staircase in the Baroque mansion of the Branicki family. The palace was known as the "Versaille of Podlasie".

← Golub-Dobrzyń. This Gothic castle from the turn of the 15th century annually hosts a knightly tournament.

Warsaw. The sculpture of the goddess Venus emerging from the bath. The Bathing Chamber of the Palace on the Isle.

Warsaw, the Castle Square. Unpretentious western facade of the Royal Castle with the Sigismund Tower and the clock on the axis. →

Pułtusk. Former castle of the bishops of Płock, currently the Polonia House.

Nieborów. The Radziwiłł family palace, 17th century Venetian globe in the library, →
in the background 18th century staircase paved with Dutch ceramic tiles.

Łódź. Neo-Baroque mansion of industrial tycoon Izrael Poznański. The edifice →→
was erected at the turn of the 20th century – garden facade.

Śmiełów. The palace, the Azure Room with frescos by Smuglewicz brothers.

Rogalin. The 18th century mansion of the Raczyński family modelled upon the Rococo and Classicism patterns, viewed from the French garden. →

Antonin. Wooden 19th century hunting mansion surrounded by spacious park with ancient oak trees. →→

Koło. Dilapidated ruins of the 14th century Gothic castle.

Gołuchów. The Castle Park: in the upper part 16th-19th century castle, in the lower part – 19th century outbuilding. →

Churches IV

Cultural purpose of temples has always been associated with symbolising the centre of the world – understood as the micro-world of the village or town. Temples sanctified space, served as a landmark and organised all things in an architectural, symbolic and spiritual sense. They served as axis mundi – the axis of the world where heaven meets earth. This cultural role of churches gave birth to their dominance both in the Polish landscape and in Poland's cultural heritage.

Initiating the portrayal of innumerable Polish churches with a description of any other temple than the Wawel Cathedral would be unseemly. There is a powerful bond between the history of this Cathedral and the past of both the castle and Poland. Two Romanesque churches originally existing on the Wawel hill vanished completely. In the 14th century current building of the Cathedral was raised on their ruins. Gradually it became encircled with multitudinous chapels, including the masterpiece of Polish Renaissance – the Sigismund Chapel. It is a burial place of Polish sovereigns, political leaders and greatest national poets.

Another of Cracow's prominent temples – St. Mary's Church on the Main Market Square – was raised at the turn of the 14th century. It is commonly deemed to be the very heart of old Cracow. The temple is adorned with the renowned Gothic altar by Veit Stoss and from its tower an hourly bugle-call has been played daily for over 600 years. The old Cracow's panorama is a magnificent skyline of church towers enthralling with multitudinous architectural styles. From Romanesque elements in St. Isidore's and St. Wojciech's churches, through classical Gothic basilicas of Franciscan and Dominican Friars, to Baroque buildings of St. Ann's and St. Peter and Paul's.

The Monastery of Jasna Góra is particularly cherished by Polish Catholics. The basilica with a Chapel of Mother of God of Częstochowa and the Paulites' Monastery are one the most frequently visited sites in Poland and the destination of innumerable pilgrimages. It is here that the Sacred Likeness of Black Madonna is exhibited. Jasna Góra was the sole speck of Poland that did not surrender to Swedish Deluge of the 17th century, which in itself intensified its exceptional meaning of a spiritual capital of Poland.

The Archsee of Gniezno towering on the Lech's Hill is a cradle of Polish Catholic Church. It is here that St. Wojciech (Adalbert) – martyr and the patron of Poland – was buried and first Polish sovereign – Bolesław Chrobry (Boleslaus the Brave) – was crowned. The Romanesque gateway to the temple is an invaluable monument of Polish early medieval art. In Poznań, on Ostrów Tumski, stands the Archsee Basilica, a seat of first Polish bishopric and a mausoleum of first Polish rulers – Mieszko I and Bolesław Chrobry. Romanesque church of St. Prokop and Romanesque pillars in the Baroque temple of the Holy Trinity, that survived in Strzelno near Gniezno, are among the oldest sacral buildings of Poland, raised along 12th century blueprints.

St. Mary's Church in Gdańsk is a pride and joy of the city and a proof of Gdańsk burghers' immense wealth. Gothic altar, St. Ann's Chapel with a statue Beautiful Madonna and a copy of Hans Memling's Last Judgement all deserve curious attention of the visitors. Pomerania also offers a Gothic Con-Cathedral in Kołobrzeg, cathedrals in Kwidzyn, Frombork and Pelplin and a Neo-Gothic cathedral of Włocławek.

Churches erected in present times deserve equal attention – particularly modernist temples of Nowa Huta: Arka (the Ark) and the Mistrzejowice church. Regrettably, the majority of Polish contemporary temples share the quality of being rather ill-looking and it would seem impossible to number them among the masterpieces of Polish architecture. Poland's biggest present-day temple is the new basilica in Licheń.

Apart from grand churches of brick or stone Polish countryside also offers charming temples made of wood. At the foothills of the Tatra Mountains one can find several Gothic wooden churches, one of them – St. Michael Archangel's church in Dębno near Nowy Targ is particularly valuable for its gorgeous 15th century wall-painting and unique, regional-style internal design. Churches of Orawka (Orawa region) and Trybsz (Spisz region) share rich ornamentation and remarkable wall-painting design. In Zakopane, apart from the simple Old Church in Kościeliska street, one can also encounter a chapel in Jaszczurówka designed by Stanisław Witkiewicz in accordance with the principles of "zakopiański" style. An old church in Rabka has been transformed into a regional museum. In Karpacz, on the other hand, one can find the original, wooden Wang church stemming from the 13th century and transported to Karpacz from its former location in Norway.

Innumerable non-Catholic temples currently existing in Poland are evidence to constant presence of religious minorities in our country. They constitute a heritage of religious diversity shared by The Republic of the Two Nations and the II Republic of Poland. For ages Poland used to be the melting pot of various ethnic and religious groups, the land of tolerance and of diverse cultural and religious traditions developing on equal rights. In Kruszyniany and Bohoniki (near Białystok) one may still find old Tatar mosques. Eastern and southern outskirts of Poland are inhabited by the members of Eastern Orthodox congregation and Greek Catholics. Numerous Orthodox churches of the region include the most renowned Polish temple of this kind erected on the mountain of Grabarka. Synagogues can still be traced in both big cities and provincial towns, the Cracow's Jewish quarter of Kazimierz has 7 of them, including the Old Synagogue that contains a museum of Jewish culture. In Silesia, Wielkopolska, Warmia and Mazury Protestant churches are relatively frequent. In Mazury one can also encounter a "molenna" – the Old Rite temple.

A church, a synagogue or an Orthodox temple have always been in the centre of local existence – in the centre of the city, village or town. It is around them that all activity took place. It still does, although many of the religious sites are a mere reminiscence of their past glory and cultural meaning.

← Trybsz in Spis region. The 16th century wooden church with Baroque-style wall-painting. Erected in 1674.

Cracow. The Wawel Castle, the Renaissance Sigismund Chapel roofed with gilded metal plates
and the Baroque Vasa Dynasty Chapel modelled upon the Sigismund Chapel.

Cracow. The interior of St. Mary's Church with an open altar pentaptych carved by Veit Stoss, the sculptor from Nurnberg. →

Rabka. Baroque organ in the church of St. Mary Magdalene.

Graboszyce near Wadowice. Single-nave wooden church from the late 16ᵗʰ century. →

Zakopane. The chapel on Jaszczurówka designed by Stanisław Witkiewicz in "Zakopiański" style.

← Orawka. St. John the Baptist Church with painted ornaments stemming from the 17ᵗʰ an the 18ᵗʰ century.

Turzańsk is a village in the Carpathian foothills forming part of the "Wooden Architecture Trail". It boasts the early ➔ ➔
19ᵗʰ-century Orthodox Church of St. Michael the Archangel. The presence of three main architectural elements
(*babiniec* area where women stand, nave and presbytery) is emphasised by the three separate roofs.

Wąchock. The Cistercian Monastery funded in 1179 to this day retains some of its original structures,
not least this Refectory building with its ornate Romanesque stonework.

Święty Krzyż. Benedictine abbey on Łysa Góra, founded in the 12th century by king Boleslaus the Wry-mouthed. →

Lublin. Gothic chapel of the Holy Trinity adorned with Byzantine and Ruthenian frescos founded by king Władysław Jagiełło.

Częstochowa. The Paulites' Monastery on Jasna Góra with the Basilica of the Assumption of the Blessed Virgin Mary →
– the object of pilgrimages and the place of worship of the Mother of God of Częstochowa.

Krzeszów. The polychromy on the ceiling of the Church of the Assumption of the Blessed Virgin Mary.
The temple is known as the "jewel of Silesian Baroque".

Karpacz. The Wang temple – 13th century church has been transported to its current location from Norway in the 19th century. ➔

Świdnica. Wooden Evangelic Church of Peace with its several-storey high galleries. It was raised in the years 1656-58. ➔➔

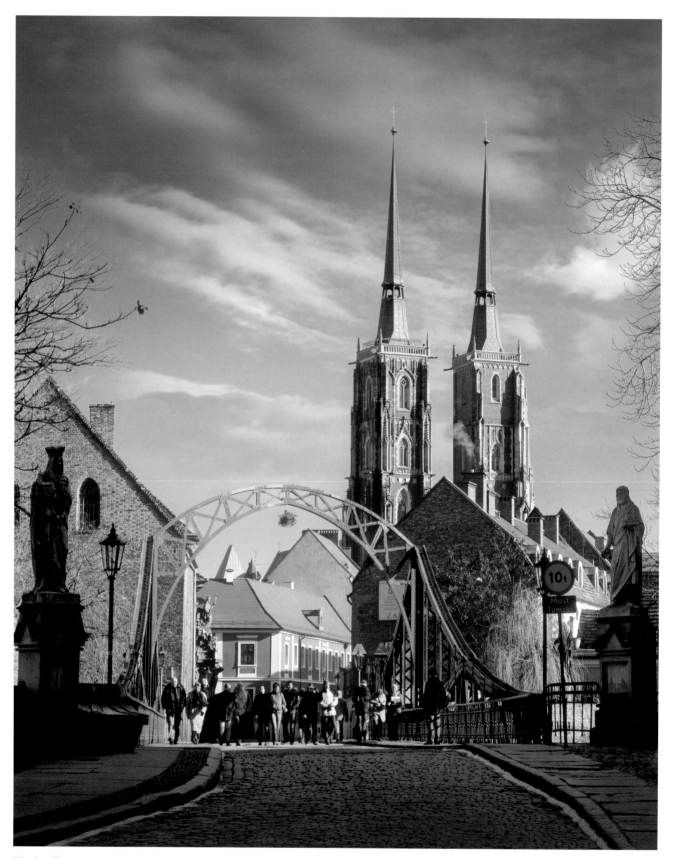

Wrocław. The two-tower Gothic Cathedral of St. John the Baptist on Ostrów Tumski island
stands dominant over the remaining buildings of the Old Town.

Trzebnica. The Church of St. Bartholomew and St. Jadwiga. The sarcophagus →
of St. Jadwiga of Silesia was completed in the years 1679-80.

Frombork. Stalls of the biggest Gothic church in Warmia region.

← Stargard. Gothic interior of the 13ᵗʰ century St. Mary's Church, ornamented with glazed multicoloured bricks.

Gdańsk. Main nave of the Gothic St. Mary's Church. In the foreground – the mid-16ᵗʰ century baptismal font. →→

Tum by Łęczyca. 12ᵗʰ century stone Romanesque Collegiate Church of the Assumption of the Blessed Virgin Mary and St. Alex.

Warsaw. The statue of Christ carrying his cross in front of the two-towered facade of the Baroque Church of the Finding of the Holy Cross. →

SVRSVM CORDA

Gniezno. The 12th century Drzwi Gnieźnieńskie (Doorway of Gniezno) – cast in bronze – depict the scenes from the life of St. Adalbert.

← Stary Licheń. Contemporary Basilica of the Blessed Virgin Mary, the largest temple in Poland, with the tower of 128 metres in height.

Rokitno. The likeness of the Holy Mother of Rokitno in the presbytery of the Church of the Mother of God Queen of Poland.

Poznań. Immense interior of the parish-church of St. Stanislaus the Bishop, with its Baroque sculptured and painted ornaments, as well as stucco work. →

Dobra near Limanowa. "Dziady śmigustne" – one of traditional customs of the Easter Monday.

← Kalwaria Zebrzydowska. Christ carrying his cross – one of the scenes of the Mystery Play. For 400 years pilgrims have annually gathered
here to witness the recreation of Christ's Via Dolorosa.

Złaków Kościelny. Colourful Corpus Christi procession. These traditional costumes stem from the Łowicz region.

Zakopane. A group of sladges with Highlanders in traditional costumes. →

Zakopane. The historic homestead of the Gąsienica-Bednarz family in Kościeliska street.

Zakopane. Wooden shrine adorned with carved ornaments and a glass painting. →

Chochołów. Private folk art museum established by a sculptor Jan Zięder in his own home. → →

Łopuszna in Podhale. Painted chest in the cottage of the Klamerus family is a background for the exhibition of folk costumes of the past.

← Ethnographic museum in Zubrzyca Górna (Orawa region). The mansion house of the Moniak family
   – former seat of the clan of "sołtys" (village administrators).

Ethnographic park in Wygiełzów. Instance of wooden architecture typical of Małopolska. → →

Tokarnia near Kielce. Original kitchen fittings in the interior of the homestead in the ethnographic
museum – the Museum of the Countryside of Kielecki Region.

Sieradzkie region. In the area one may encounter such thatched cottages still inhabited. →

Russów. Ethnographic exhibition in the manor house park – the interior of a peasant's cottage.

Dziekanowice. 19th century windmills from the vicinity of Gniezno, Dutch tower and paltrock mills, in the Ethnographic Museum of Wielkopolska. ➔

CHRISTIAN PARMA
photography

MACIEJ KRUPA
text

BOGNA PARMA
captions of photographs

STANISŁAWA KOSIOREK
Polish Folk Art
example of a folk-art papercut

ANETA CZARNECKA
BOGNA PARMA
layout

ANNA CZAJKOWSKA (CLEAR EYES TRANSLATORS)
translation

WYDAWNICTWO PARMA PRESS
ANETA CZARNECKA
OLGA BARANOWSKA
ELIZA DZIENIO
dtp

Wydawnictwo PARMA PRESS
05 270 Marki, al. Józefa Piłsudskiego 189 b
+48 22/ 781 16 48, 781 16 49
e-mail: wydawnictwo@parmapress.com.pl
www.parmapress.com.pl
publisher

ISBN 978-83-7777-099-3

Marki 2017

cover photo: Zaborów. This Eclectic-style palace was built in 1903 for banker Leon Feliks Goldsztand.
photo on the title page: The Fryderyk Chopin Monument in Warsaw's Łazienki Park.

Cracow. The most famous Polish commercial gallery of art presents paintings for sale along the inner side of defensive wall at Floriańska Gate.